Christopher Browne

MARLO
and the Dinosaurs

BALZER + BRAY
An Imprint of HarperCollinsPublishers

Help Marlo find these friends
as they explore the world of the dinosaurs.

Balzer + Bray is an imprint of HarperCollins Publishers.

Marlo and the Dinosaurs

ISBN 978-0-06-244115-7

The artist used pen and watercolor on paper, colored digitally to create the illustrations for this book.
Typography by Dana Fritts
17 18 19 20 21 SCP 10 9 8 7 6 5 4 3 2 1
❖
First Edition

To Caroline, the center of my universe

Marlo awoke from his afternoon
nap to a very strange sight.

He decided to investigate.

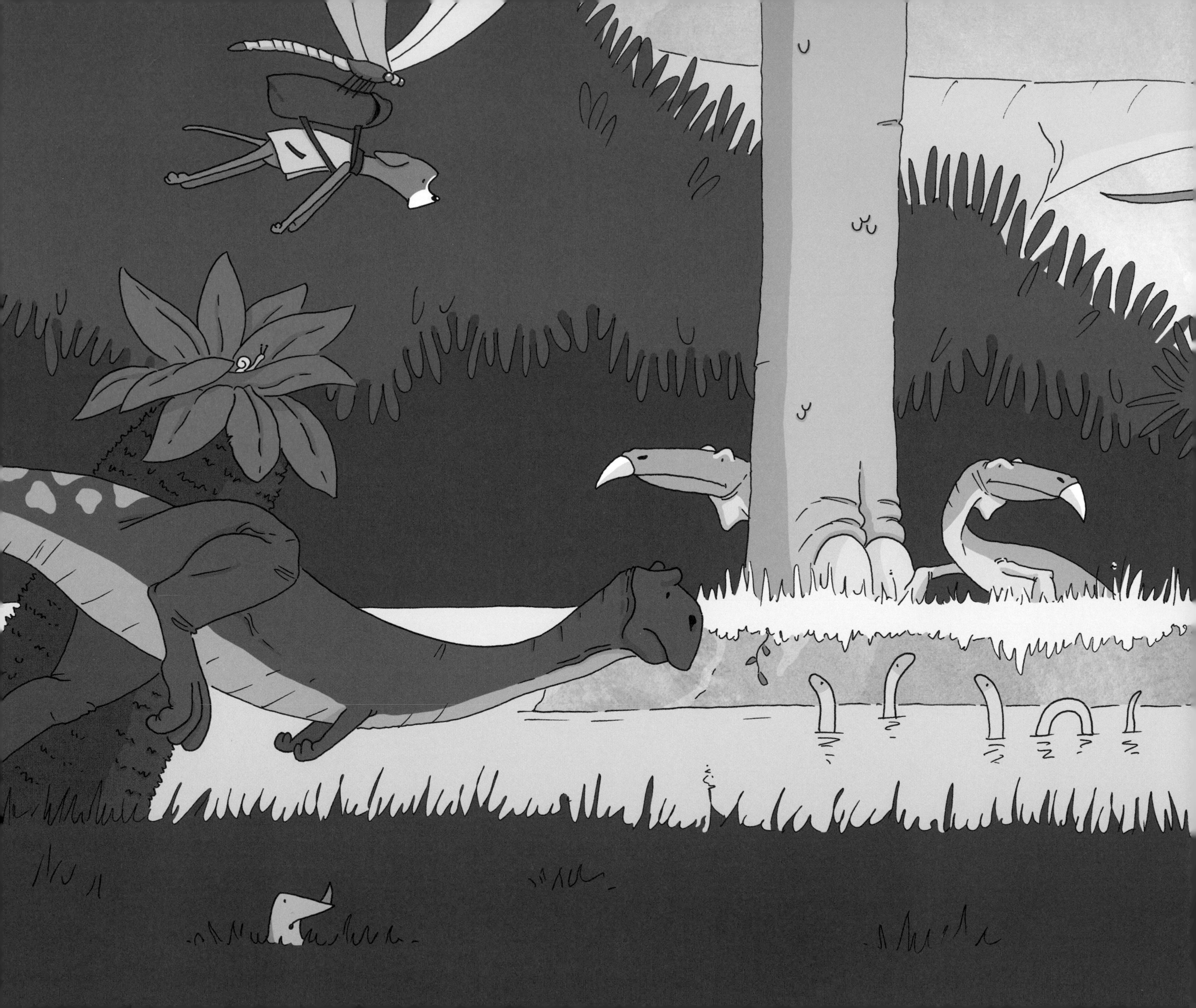

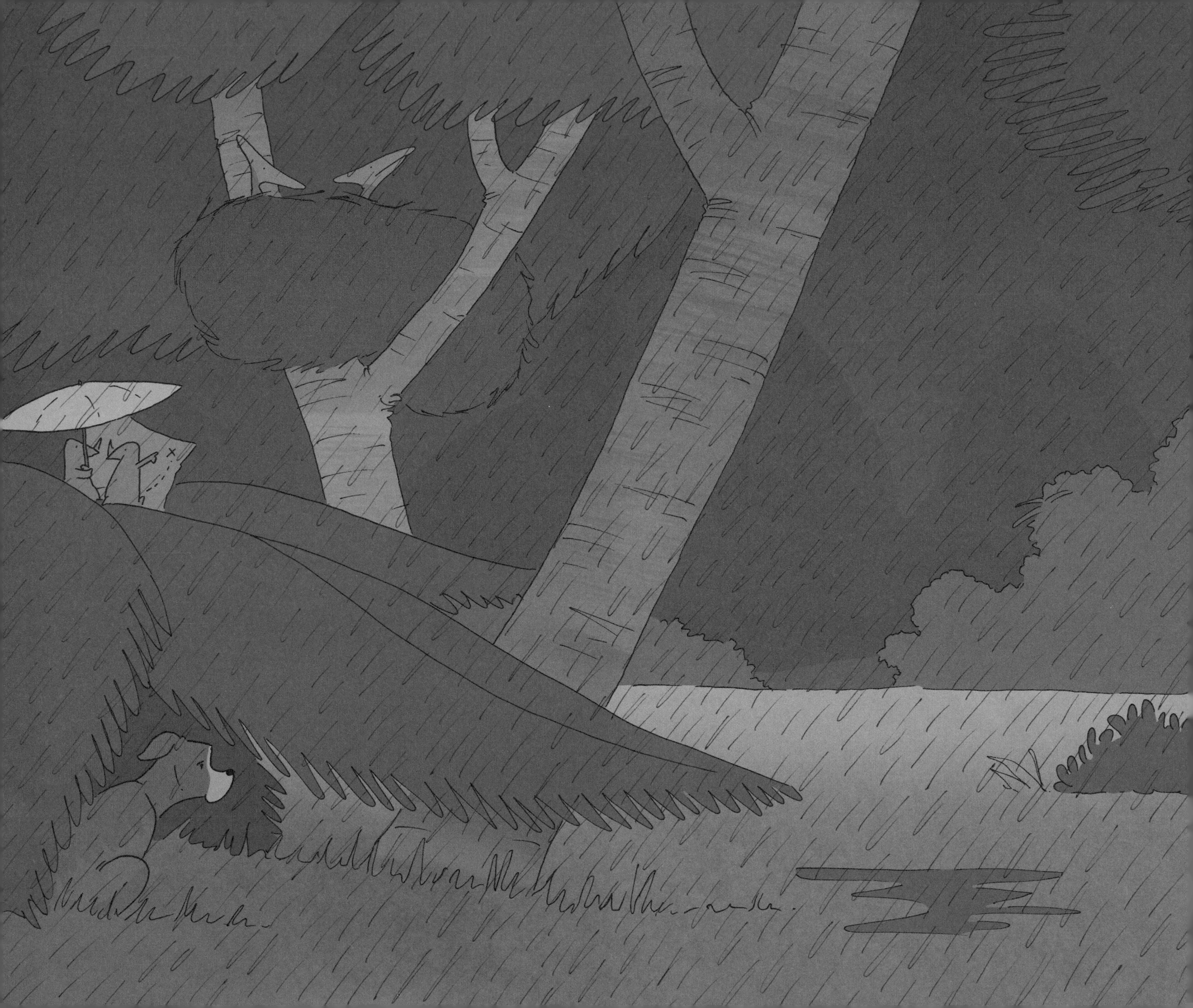

"Marlo! Time for a walk."

"Marlo?"